KING JOHN, THE MAGNA CARTA AND DEMOCRACY

History for Kids Books
Chidren's European History

BABY PROFESSOR
EDUCATION KIDS

Speedy Publishing LLC

40 E. Main St. #1156

Newark, DE 19711

www.speedypublishing.com

Copyright 2017

In this book, we're going to talk about King John and the Magna Carta. So, let's get right to it!

King John

WHAT WAS THE MAGNA CARTA?

The Magna Carta, also called the Great Charter, was a very important document that was signed in the Middle Ages. King John of England was put under pressure to sign it in 1215 AD. The barons in England were rebelling against his rule and they wanted more rights.

By signing this document, the King changed the monarchy's powers. The document also changed the rights of the citizens of England as well as the amount of influence the members of Parliament had on the country.

King John signing the Magna Carta

The Magna Carta replica

King John was considered to be one of the worst Kings in history and his barons wanted to force him into following the law. The Magna Carta was eventually written into English law. The Magna Carta became a symbol of liberty. Its underlying philosophy was that everyone should follow the law, even those in positions of power or government leaders.

Today, you can read the text of the Magna Carta online. Much of it has to do with the customs of feudal lands in Medieval Times, but its basic purpose shines through. The Magna Carta influenced several other important documents including the Declaration of Independence as well as the United States Constitution and Bill of Rights.

Writing the Declaration of Independence

Stephen Langton

WHAT WAS THE PURPOSE OF THE MAGNA CARTA?

Members of the Church, primarily Stephen Langton who was archbishop, and the barons who were rebelling, wrote the text for the Magna Carta. Its purpose was to decrease the amount of power that the King had. The barons wanted him to go back to the laws that were in place before the Normans had invaded England.

The Magna Carta was written as a list of contractual statements designating that the King would use the customs and laws already in place for feudal law in his dealings with his subjects. The "Articles of the Barons" as the document was originally called, was their effort at getting the King to stop his tyrannical behavior, especially when it was causing ordinary citizens undue suffering.

Magna Carta of King John, AD 1215

WHAT EVENTS LED UP TO THE SIGNING OF THE MAGNA CARTA?

The barons of England were a force to be reckoned with. After all, without the assistance of the barons, the King couldn't run the country. They gave the King funds and soldiers to protect French territories that were now in the hands of the English. It was traditional for the King to discuss his plans with the barons before levying any new taxes.

The barons would be asked to help gather these funds so they would need to be in agreement that the taxes were important. Traditionally, the King would also ask for their advice before requesting additional soldiers since it would be the barons' responsibility to recruit, enlist, organize, and train these soldiers. These established customs were already part of the Feudal System that had been used for centuries.

King John

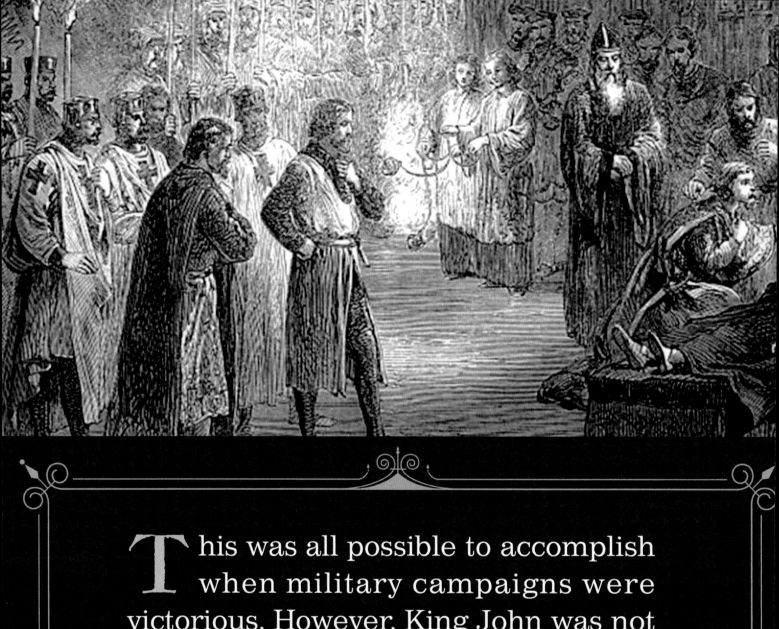

This was all possible to accomplish when military campaigns were victorious. However, King John was not a successful war strategist. His battles abroad had brought nothing but defeat.

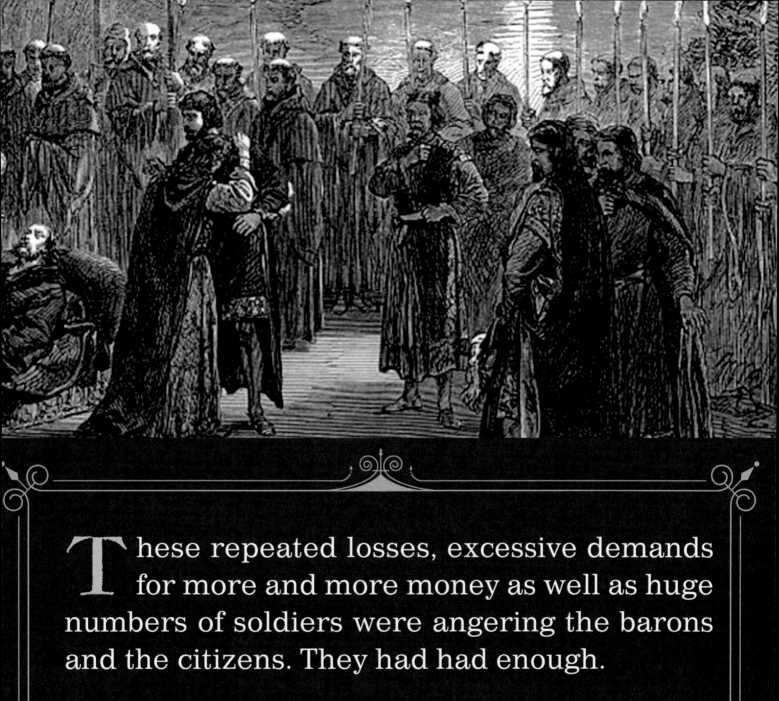

These repeated losses, excessive demands for more and more money as well as huge numbers of soldiers were angering the barons and the citizens. They had had enough.

King John was not successful in keeping lands in the north part of France that England had previously owned. His coffers were empty in 1204 and he decided to increase taxes in order to supply himself and his court with money. He did this without consulting the barons. This was in direct violation of feudal laws. The barons had been pushed beyond their breaking point.

In addition to angering his barons and his subjects, he had also been having battles with the Roman Catholic Church. The Church was very powerful in those days, so he was putting himself in a weakened position by doing this.

EVENTS TIMELINE

KING JOHN'S CORONATION AND DISAGREEMENTS WITH THE CHURCH

In 1198 AD, King Richard died and King John took the throne in 1199.

In 1205 AD, Pope Innocent III had an argument with King John. The Pope wanted Stephen Langton for the title of Archbishop of Canterbury. However, King John was against having Langton.

Pope Innocent III

Stephen Langton

In 1209 AD, after this argument had still not been resolved, the Pope had had enough. He decided that he would excommunicate the King. According to Church law this meant that if King John passed away he would not be admitted to heaven.

The Pope also put some restrictions on the way the churches in England were performing their services. The ordinary citizens and parishioners were very alarmed that they would also lose their ability to get into heaven due to King John's actions. They wanted him to comply with the Pope's wishes so there wouldn't be retaliation from the Pope.

INNOCENT III.

Stephen Langton

King John gave in and agreed to Stephen Langton as Archbishop of Canterbury. However, after four years, the Pope wanted to make sure that King John felt his wrath. He ordered him to pay the papacy enormous sums of money.

TAXES ON THE PEOPLE

King John had no intention of paying the Pope out of his own reserve. He began to tax his subjects. His taxes were so huge that he destroyed their economies and communities. For those who didn't pay, the punishment was severe and quick. There was no room for justice or reconsideration.

In 1212 AD, King John started to levy additional taxes on his barons. Through his poor war strategy he had lost the conquests of Anjou and Aquitaine as well as Poitou. He wanted to regain these lands and needed money and men.

However, he had pushed the situation too far and the payments he was trying to obtain were too oppressive. The barons began to question his practices and they started to quarrel openly with the King.

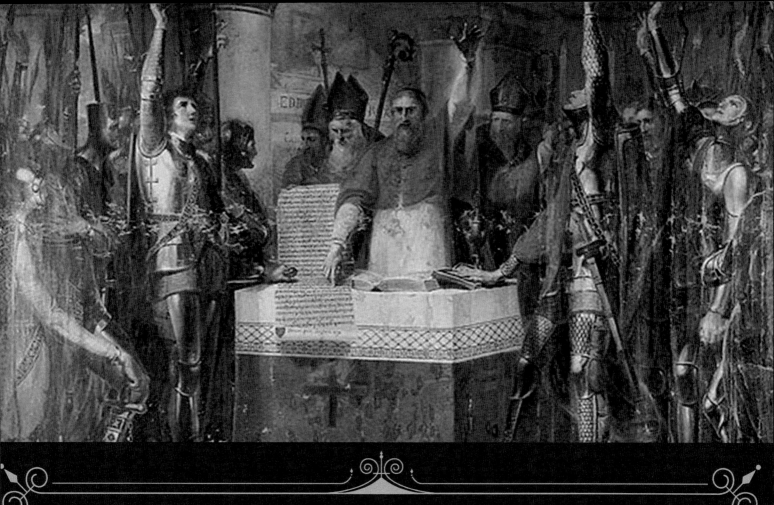

To avoid paying these taxes, the barons decided it might be time for further action and they aligned themselves with Stephen Langton who was now in the powerful position of Archbishop of Canterbury.

King John's Castle

In 1214 AD, more losses meant that King John returned home asking once again for more funds and troops. The barons didn't want to respond to these requests.

THE CREATION OF THE "ARTICLES OF THE BARONS"

The barons felt that the King was out of control. He needed to go back and govern by the previous English laws that had been in place before William the Conqueror and the other Norman kings had been on the throne. The country prior to the Norman invasion had had many more freedoms before the power had been taken from the Anglo-Saxons.

William the Conqueror

King John's Castle

By January 1215, the barons had stated all their demands in the document entitled the "Articles of the Barons." Now that they were clear on their intentions, they began to organize to get the King to sign off on their demands. In May of 1215 AD, they took over the city of London. This gave them a strong position to leverage their power and get the King's cooperation.

THE KING IS CORNERED

The barons got ready in their full armor and then boxed King John into a corner in June of 1215. He was caught by surprise and had to agree to a meeting with them at Runnymede.

Magna Carta Memorial, Runnymede

There wasn't much the King could do. They were forcing his hand. He signed the document and used the Royal Seal to close it up. The barons thought that he would honor his signature and they renewed their oath to him.

DECEIT AND REBELLION

King John just signed the agreement because he was forced to do so. He had no intention of paying attention to it. Soon the barons realized this and went to war with him beginning in 1215.

Prince Louis VIII of France took advantage of the unrest and decided to invade England. He went to London and King John's barons supported him as the King. He took over, even though he was never formally proclaimed king, and King John didn't relinquish the throne.

Louis VIII

King John's tomb

When King John died a few months later, the barons quickly turned on the Prince. King John had a son who was nine years old. The barons gave their support to him and he was crowned King Henry III.

WHY WAS THE MAGNA CARTA IMPORTANT?

The Magna Carta was important because it was the beginning of handing power to the people instead of to just a few rulers. It changed the way people perceived the power of the monarchy.

King Henry III

Magna Carta

It changed the workings of the interaction between the Parliament and the King and gave certain civil rights to the subjects of the land.

It showed that the power of a leader could be curbed by the strength of a supported document.

Many documents throughout the world have been influenced by the spirit and philosophy of the Magna Carta. When English settlers traveled to America they adopted the same types of civil rights that had been outlined in the Magna Carta. Because of this, the Magna Carta influenced the Declaration of Independence, the Constitution, and the Bill of Rights.

Signing of Declaration of Independence

Awesome! Now you know more about King John, the Magna Carta, and how it influenced democracy. You can find more European History books from Baby Professor by searching the website of your favorite book retailer.